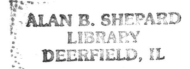

The SANTA FE TRAIL

by
LINDA THOMPSON

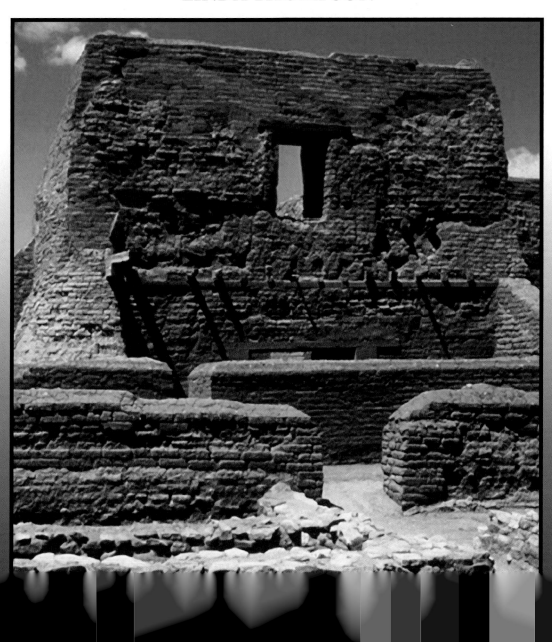

www.rourkepublishing.com

PHOTO CREDITS:
Courtesy Bureau of Land Management: pages 9, 10, 21, 32; Courtesy Denver Public Library, Western History Collection: pages 14, 32; Courtesy Detroit Publishing Company: pages 11, 40; Courtesy Northwestern University Library, Edward S. Curtis Collection: pages 7, 27; Courtesy National Museum of Natural History, The Smithsonian Institution James E. Taylor Album: page 37; Courtesy Library of Congress, Prints and Photographs Division: pages 16, 24, 25, 31, 32, 33, 39; Courtesy National Oceanographic and Atmospheric Administration: page 19; Courtesy National Parks Service: Title, 19, 28, 29, 36; Courtesy Nebraska State Historical Society: page 31; Courtesy Ering and Reilah Jones: pages 23, 27, 42; Courtesy Rohm Padilla: 4-5, 12-13, 14-15, 24, 41; Courtesy U.S. Fish and Wildlife Services: page 15; Courtesy U.S. Geological Survey: page 17; Courtesy U.S. Military Photo Archives: page 19.

SPECIAL NOTE: Further information about people's names shown in the text in bold can be found on page 43. More information about glossary terms in bold in the text can be found on pages 46 and 47.

DESIGN AND LAYOUT: ROHM PADILLA

Library of Congress Cataloging-In-Publication Data

Thompson, Linda, 1941-
    The Santa Fe Trail / Linda Thompson.
        p. cm. -- (The expansion of America)
    Includes bibliographical references and index.
    ISBN 1-59515-226-1
    1. Santa Fe National Historic Trail--Juvenile literature. I. Title. II.
Series: Thompson, Linda, 1941-   Expansion of America.
    F786.T46 2004
    978--dc22

                            2004010034

TITLE PAGE IMAGE
Ruins at Pecos that are now a national park. Pecos was the site of a pueblo and one of the last stops on the Santa Fe Trail.

TABLE OF CONTENTS

Only 20 years after it became independent, the United States gained a region that doubled the country's size. And barely 50 years later, it reached across immense plains and towering mountain ranges to touch the Pacific Ocean. How it grew so fast in such a short time is still an amazing tale. One thing that promoted this growth was the strong desire of people to trade with each other.

PACIFIC OCEAN

OREGON TERRITORY 1846

ESTABLISHED 1818

CEDED BY MEXICO 1848

LOUISIANA PURCHASE 1803

GADSDEN PURCHASE 1853

TEXAS ANNEXED 1845

"...from sea to shining sea."

When the year 1803 began, the United States of America had only 17 states and one large **territory** surrounding the Great Lakes. Most of the five and a half million Americans lived along the eastern edge of a huge undeveloped continent. Georgia was the southernmost state and the western border of the country was the Mississippi River. But by the end of 1803, President Thomas Jefferson had purchased the vast and unknown Louisiana Territory. More land was quickly acquired. In 1846, defining the boundary with Canada made the Pacific Northwest part of the United States. By 1848, the country had added Florida and California, as well as Texas and the Southwest. In 1853, with the Gadsden Purchase (southern Arizona and New Mexico), the **continental** United States looked as it does today in size and shape, not counting Alaska.

ATLANTIC OCEAN

UNITED STATES PRIOR TO 1803

In less than 100 years the shape of the continental United States had expanded from the Atlantic Ocean, across mountains and plains, to the Pacific Ocean.

CEDED BY SPAIN 1819

The first paths across North America were formed by migrating animal herds and the Native Americans who followed and hunted them.
(Below) a Southwest Native drawing of a deer

The challenge of exploring all of this newly acquired territory was immense. But Americans were equal to the challenge. By 1869, a **transcontinental** railroad linked the 3,500 miles (5,633 km) or more of wilderness between the two coasts. The land suddenly became more accessible to explorers, settlers, and people bringing supplies and mail. And there were nearly six times as many Americans as when the century had begun. People had not only explored and settled much of the new land, but also had made it easier to transport goods and communicate with each other "from sea to shining sea."

Long before the railroads came, a network of trails had begun to connect the far-flung parts of the continent. These trails were begun by many tribes of Native Americans who had inhabited the country for more than 10,000 years before Europeans and others arrived. Natives tended to follow trails made by animals such as deer, elk, and buffalo. These trails marked the most convenient routes across mountains, rivers, and prairies. These routes later became the well-known trails for exploring and settling the West. One of the oldest was the Santa Fe Trail, which ran from Independence, Missouri, to Santa Fe, New Mexico, a distance of about 900 miles (1,450 km).

Apache men on horseback, discussing which trail to use

Unlike the later Oregon and California trails, the Santa Fe Trail was not created by settlers heading west, but by merchants seeking to trade. For many years it linked Mexico and the United States, which were not always on the best of terms with each other. Yet even when those countries were at war, this **artery** of trade remained open. Women and children, as well as men, risked their lives to make the long and difficult journey from a familiar world into a foreign one, and some chose the strange new world as their home.

Some trappers and frontiersmen partnered with Natives for help getting around areas that they did not know.

Chapter II: THE ORIGINS OF THE SANTA FE TRAIL

Santa Fe is the oldest capital city in the United States. The Spanish, who were exploring northward from Mexico, founded it in 1610. Santa Fe and all of Nuevo Mexico (New Mexico), which was much larger than it is now, belonged to Mexico, a province of Spain. The Spanish at first supplied Santa Fe and other villages in New Mexico from Mexico City, 1,500 miles (2,414 km) away, using an ancient trail called El Camino Real (the Royal Highway). By the early 1700s, the **caravans** had begun forming at Chihuahua, Mexico, shortening the trip to only about 350 miles (563 km).

Aerial view of Interstate 25, a railroad track, and the old El Camino Real National Historic Trail. Established in 1598, this trail from Mexico City to Santa Fe provided vital communications and trade between Mexico and the frontier lands of New Mexico.

Taos Pueblo with the snow-capped Sangre de Cristo Mountains in the background

Although the founding of the Santa Fe Trail is said to have been 1821, when trade was firmly established between the United States and New Mexico, sections of the trail are much older. **Taos Pueblo**, 75 miles (121 km) north of Santa Fe, had been a center of trade between **Pueblo** peoples and Plains tribes such as the **Apache**, **Ute**, and **Comanche** for several centuries. One of the trails made by these traders became the western section of the Santa Fe Trail, running between the Arkansas River in present-day Kansas and the Rio Grande River, near Taos, New Mexico.

The Santa Fe Trail sometimes followed rivers such as the Rio Grande (left) and the Arkansas River (right).

American merchants met with obstacles when attempting to trade with Mexico. After creating a vast **empire** in the New World, Spain needed money to govern it. So the Spanish king **taxed** all trade goods heavily. To ensure that the taxes would be paid, Spain let United States merchandise enter Mexico only through the port of Veracruz, far to the south on the Gulf of Mexico. Goods bound for Santa Fe, to the north, had to be carried 2,000 miles (3,220 km) by oxcarts or mule-drawn wagons. Taxes and transportation costs made the merchandise extremely expensive once it arrived in Santa Fe. For example, fabric for clothing that cost pennies per yard (.91 m) in Boston sold for two or three dollars a yard in Santa Fe. One hundred pounds (45.5 kg) of flour cost less than a dollar in Franklin, Missouri, but two dollars in Santa Fe.

A colorized photo of an ox-drawn cart from Chihuahua, Mexico, taken in the late 1800s. Carts traveling north would have been even larger and required more oxen to pull their cargo.

EQUIVALENTS

To compare 19th century prices with today's dollars, two dollars in 1808 would be $31 today. A wagon was bought in St. Louis in 1822 for $150 ($2,280 today) and sold in Santa Fe for $750 ($11,400 in today's dollars).

The isolation of Santa Fe and the resulting high prices at first discouraged American traders.

COLORADO

PIKES PEAK

PUEBLO

OLD BENT'S FORT

BENT'S NEW FORT

RATON PASS

RATON

TAOS

OK

TX

SANTA FE

WAGON MOUND

FORT UNION

LAS VEGAS

GLORIETA PASS

PECOS RUINS

NEW MEXICO

THE SANTA FE TRAIL

Many early explorers felt the profit to be made was worth the risk of traveling along the Santa Fe Trail.

But some understood that if a shorter trade route to Santa Fe could be found, excellent profits could be made.

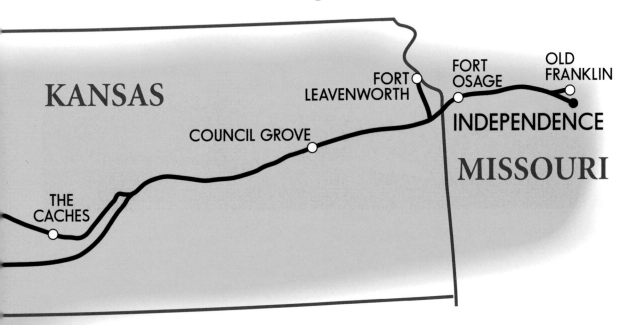

At the time of the Louisiana Purchase, the most westerly American settlement was the frontier town of Franklin on the Missouri River. In 1806, the United States government sent **Zebulon Pike** to explore the southern part of the new territory. (In 1804, **Meriwether Lewis** and **William Clark** led a major exploration into the northern and western sections.) Pike followed the Arkansas River to the Rio Grande, where Spanish troops arrested him, accusing him of being a spy. He and his men were taken to Santa Fe and Chihuahua, then escorted to the border and released a few months later. Pike published the first report in English about a possible route to Santa Fe in 1810. He was also the first to describe the high prices there.

Early caravans were often attacked and raided by groups of Native Americans or taken prisoner by Spanish soldiers.

Eager to sell their goods for such prices, some traders from Franklin set out with a merchandise caravan in 1812. They traveled along the Arkansas River almost as far as present-day Pueblo, Colorado, then followed an Indian trail over Raton Pass in the **Sangre de Cristo Mountains**. When they reached Santa Fe, they were arrested and their goods were taken. They spent eight years in a Chihuahua prison and were released in 1820 upon orders from the King of Spain.

Sangre de Cristo Mountains, Taos, New Mexico

The high value of a beaver pelt made it highly valuable to hunters and trappers.

Meanwhile, hunters and trappers were also discovering the Sangre de Cristo Mountains. They found the rivers and streams full of beaver, an animal highly sought after for its fur. One beaver pelt would bring six dollars in St. Louis, Missouri, the same as a buffalo robe–but a horse could carry many more beaver skins than buffalo robes. The French, whose American headquarters was New Orleans, were the most skilled fur trappers in the New World. A party led by **Auguste Chouteau** collected $30,000 worth of pelts. But when they stopped at Taos for supplies, the men were arrested and imprisoned and their furs were taken away.

After that, American trappers mostly stayed on the north side of the border. But in 1821, a Franklin trader, **William Becknell**, took a trading party into Spanish territory. They crossed Raton Pass north of Taos, and continued to the Canadian River, where they came upon a small troop of Mexican soldiers. Expecting to be arrested, Becknell was surprised when the troopers welcomed his party and suggested that they continue to Santa Fe with their merchandise. It seemed that Mexico had just won its independence from Spain. Now, with the high Spanish **tariffs** gone, the Mexicans were eager to trade with the United States. Becknell opened a trading post in Santa Fe that operated for more than 40 years. He is known as the "Father of the Santa Fe Trail."

Mexican soldiers encouraged trade once the country gained its independence from Spain.

THE CACHES

A famous landmark on the Santa Fe Trail, "**The Caches**," was created when an 1822 caravan left Franklin late and was caught by winter snows at the Arkansas River. The traders, **James Baird** and **Samuel Chambers**, were forced to bury their merchandise in deep holes on an island because many of their pack animals had died of cold and hunger. In spring, they went to Taos, bought horses and returned, dug up their goods, and continued to Santa Fe. The empty pits, or caches, could still be seen as late as 1970. They marked the spot where travelers left the river to take the Cimarron Cutoff.

Historic trail marker designating the location of "The Caches"

This skeleton shows how harsh the effects of the desert climate can be, especially with the lack of water.

In 1822, Becknell led a second caravan of 22 men to Santa Fe, where the traders sold their goods at a huge profit. To avoid taking its three wagons over the 7,834-foot (2,388-m) high Raton Pass, this party had taken a shortcut, leaving the Arkansas River about where Dodge City, Kansas, now stands. But this route forced the men and livestock to walk across a 60-mile (97-km) wide desert with no water. Becknell's party was saved when some of the men shot a buffalo, slit open its abdomen, and drank the water inside. Its tracks led them to the Cimarron River. Refreshed, they continued on to Santa Fe. Their route, which became known as the "Cimarron Cutoff," trimmed about 100 miles (160 km) off the journey.

(Left) flooding in a Missouri town in 1903. (Above) this marker is what is left of old Franklin, Missouri.

After Franklin, Missouri, was flooded in the 1820s, Independence, founded in 1827, became the eastern end of the Santa Fe Trail. Independence is just east of present-day Kansas City, Missouri.

The western end of the trail is shown in this drawing of Santa Fe by a soldier stationed there in the mid 1800s.

Chapter III: THE TRAIL'S HEYDAY

In 1824, Missouri, which had recently become a state but was suffering through a **recession**, began promoting trading in Santa Fe as a way to bring money into the state. **Thomas Hart Benton**, a United States Senator from Missouri, portrayed his state as a "gateway to the West." He sponsored legislation to survey the Santa Fe Trail, and in 1825 President **James Monroe** signed it into law. It provided $10,000 for marking the route and $20,000 for making peace with the Indians.

The survey was completed as far as Taos, a distance of 740 miles (1,191 km). The party negotiated peace treaties with the **Osage** and **Kansas** tribes, allowing passage through their lands. The surveyors marked the trail with mounds of dirt. Unfortunately, the government failed to publish the survey results and within the next few years, the mounds had washed away. Also, the journal of **George Sibley**, a member of the survey party, was lost and not published until 1952. So the Santa Fe Trail never became an official road, and each caravan had to seek its way by following the deep ruts of earlier wagons. These ruts are still visible in a number of places along the trail.

These wagon ruts in Colorado have been etched in the stone and are still visible today.

The main benefit of the 1825-1827 survey was to ease relations with the eastern tribes, but further to the west and south the **Pawnee, Cheyenne, Kiowa**, and Comanche continued to attack trading parties. Many caravans lost their horses and mules, and the survivors had to abandon or bury their goods and silver and set out on foot. They suffered cold, hunger, thirst, and extreme hardship in these cases. Traders began to join their parties with Mexican hunters and friendly Indians to have a better chance against the raiding tribes.

The treaty place with the Osage, about 150 miles (241 km) southwest of Independence, was called Council Grove. By 1831, it had become a **rendezvous** point for caravans setting out on the Santa Fe Trail. Because of increased Mexican tariffs and the need for safety, small caravans had little chance of making it to Santa Fe and selling their goods profitably. Mexican **customs** officials might set the value of merchandise at 130 percent of the cost paid in Missouri, and the tax had to be paid on the higher amount. The result was that fewer traders made the journey but caravans became larger. In 1824, for instance, 80 traders carried goods worth about $35,000, but in 1827 only 50 traders took $90,000 worth of merchandise to Santa Fe. These caravans typically had 130 men and 60 or 70 wagons pulled by oxen. The men rode mules or horses or walked alongside the wagons.

Because of the high taxes and risk of robbery, the size of caravans and wagons slowly increased along the trail.

In the 1830s, some caravan leaders began choosing the northern mountain route through Taos and avoiding the desert completely. This route added about 100 miles (160 km) to the trip. Large caravans could travel only about 12 to 15 miles (19 to 24 km) a day, so the entire journey, nearly 900 miles (1,448 km), might take between two and three months.

By the time this cabin was built in the late 1800s, Council Grove was an established settlement.

THIS LOG CABIN RESEMBLES ONE DESCRIBED AS THE INGALLS HOME IN LITTLE HOUSE ON THE PRAIRIE. A CLAIM WAS NOT FILED BECAUSE THE LAND WAS PART OF THE OSAGE DIMINISHED RESERVE. THE OSAGE SIGNED THE TREATY SELLING THE LAND TO THE GOVERNMENT ON SEPTEMBER 10 TH 1870 THE FAMILY HOME WAS LISTED AS THE 89 TH RESIDENCE OF RUTLAND TOWNSHIP IN THE 1870 U.S. CENSUS, AND THE FAMILY LIVED HERE ABOUT ONE YEAR. IN HER BOOK LAURA TOLD OF BUILDING THE CABIN, OF ENCOUNTERS WITH INDIANS OF GOING TO INDEPENDENCE FOR SUPPLIES AND OF Dr. TANNS TREATING THE FAMILY MEMBERS FOR FEVER 'N'AGUE' Dr. TANNS GRAVE IS IN MOUNT HOPE CEMETERY IN INDEPENDENCE. ERECTED 1977

MISSOURI MULE

The famous "Missouri Mule" owes its creation to the Santa Fe Trail.

Stephen Cooper led a trading caravan to Santa Fe in 1823, and upon returning to Franklin he brought 400 "jacks" (Spanish donkeys) and "jennies" (**offspring** of a male horse and female donkey). The Spanish donkeys and mules were small and very strong. Missouri farmers used them to create an entire mule industry.

(Left) this statue depicting a Missouri mule stands outside the present-day Santa Fe Plaza in New Mexico.

(Below) President Andrew Jackson

Because of frequent Indian attacks, traders called for military protection, and in 1829 the new president, **Andrew Jackson**, ordered four **companies** of soldiers to escort caravans as far as the Mexican border. An 1829 expedition led by 30-year-old **Charles Bent** was the first to be escorted. But military support dropped off after a few years, and traders had to protect themselves. By traveling in a compact group and gathering the wagons together at night, they improved their chances of survival. Each **division** of a caravan had a **lieutenant** who rode in advance, checking out rough spots in the road. He supervised the wagon formations at night. Wagons were placed in a square, circle, or oval, front wheel to rear wheel, and the wheels were sometimes chained together. Thus, a temporary **stockade** was formed and the livestock could be driven inside.

Caravans protected themselves by gathering together at night.

Friendships that grew out of the 1829 caravan influenced the history of the Southwest. Charles Bent and his friend, **Ceran St. Vrain**, formed a trading company that became a strong economic force in New Mexico. **William Bent**, Charles's younger brother, and **Kit Carson** also became fast friends. In 1829, both were only 20 years old. Both men later played a part in subduing the Indians of the region. In 1830, Charles Bent and St. Vrain forged a new route across the Kansas plains. It was longer than Becknell's Cimarron Cutoff but had several advantages. There was less sand for the wagons to bog down in and fewer days to travel without water. The Bent-St. Vrain Company prospered and sent trading expeditions as far south as Chihuahua.

JEDEDIAH SMITH

Jedediah Smith spent his early twenties winning fame as an explorer, Indian trader, and sharpshooter west of the Missouri. In 1831, on a trading mission across the Cimarron Desert, he scouted ahead for water and disappeared. Later, his brother found Jedediah's pistols for sale in Santa Fe and learned that Comanches had attacked and killed him. But Smith had fought so hard, killing 13 of them before he died, that the Comanches had given him a funeral ceremony usually reserved for a chief.

Photo of an Apsaroke party after a successful horse raid

BENT AND OXEN

Charles Bent and his brother, William, were already familiar with trapping and trading ways. Charles noted that Indians were not interested in stealing oxen. Also, oxen plodded slowly along without needing to rest as much as mules did. His discovery that oxen were superior over difficult terrain influenced other traders. Within a few years, oxen outnumbered mules four to one on the Santa Fe Trail.

Oxen with a yoke around their necks

Caravans were protected by **mountain men**, who were better fighters than soldiers and had more knowledge of Indian ways. Some of these men were Jedediah Smith, William Sublette, David Jackson, and Tom Fitzpatrick. William Bent had always been interested in Native Americans, spoke a few Native languages, and eventually married Owl Woman, the daughter of Gray Thunder, a Cheyenne medicine man. Bent's friend, Yellow Wolf, a Cheyenne chief, urged him to build a trading post along the Santa Fe Trail's mountain route. In 1834, Bent built a military fort at the current location of La Junta, Colorado. Today, this is known as Bent's Old Fort National Historical Site.

Bent's Old Fort, Colorado

BENT'S FORT

Bent's Fort was 178 by 137 feet (54 m by 42 m) and had 4-foot (1.2-m) thick **adobe** walls. Its only entrance was a square tunnel with a huge wood and iron door. Indians could trade through small windows without coming inside the fort. The building had **turrets** on four corners and cannons mounted in a **watchtower** above the tunnel. The fort could store two years worth of provisions and trade goods. It was not attacked before 1847 because William Bent dealt honestly with Native Americans and they respected him.

A modern re-creation of a prairie schooner

In 1839, Governor **Manuel Armijo** of Mexico increased taxes on wagonloads of United States goods to an astounding $500 per wagon. This meant traders had to build larger wagons to make the caravans profitable. Huge "**prairie schooners**" were built that required as many as 30 oxen to pull them. Charles and William Bent and others who could afford to take this step benefited, but many went out of business. Bent's Fort was the largest American trading center west of St. Louis. In 1846, the annual spring caravan left Missouri with 414 prairie schooners, 8,000 draft animals, and more than 500 men. Commercial traffic on the Santa Fe Trail was beginning to reach its peak.

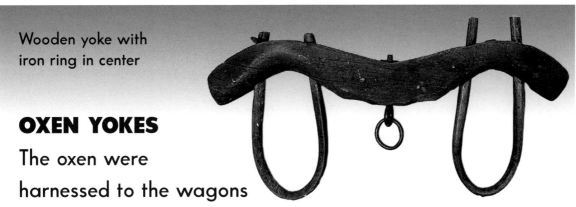

Wooden yoke with iron ring in center

OXEN YOKES

The oxen were harnessed to the wagons with huge wooden **yokes**. One curved yoke sat on the necks of two oxen, just behind the horns. A curved wooden bow went around each animal's neck and was held in place with wooden or metal pins. The wagon **tongue** was attached to an iron ring, which hung from the center of each yoke.

Miners heading west with two oxen yoked to their cart

Christopher "Kit" Carson, wearing suit jacket, vest, and tie

KIT CARSON AND BUFFALO MEAT

To feed several hundred employees and guests, Bent needed 1,000 pounds (454 kg) of buffalo meat a day. But buffalo were becoming scarce by the late 1830s, and as they disappeared Indians became more hostile toward the traders. In 1838, Kit Carson made a deal with Bent to supply the fort with buffalo meat. Because Kit and his "Carson Men" had a reputation of "strong medicine" with Native groups, they succeeded in their job without being attacked.

Large numbers of Americans had settled in Texas while it was part of Mexico. They had rebelled against Mexican rule in 1836 and established the Republic of Texas, which was recognized by the United States but not by Mexico. Border disputes led to a **skirmish** between Mexican and United States troops in 1846, which caused the United States to

declare war on Mexico. This was the Mexican War. President James Polk sent an army under Zachary Taylor to fight in the south. From the north, Brigadier General **Stephen Watts Kearny** marched his "Army of the West" over the Santa Fe Trail with the goal of capturing Santa Fe.

General (later President) Zachary Taylor

Illustration of U.S. Cavalry in a battle with Mexican troops

When Kearny's troops reached Santa Fe, Governor Manuel Armijo abandoned the town and fled south. He had been persuaded not to fight by an American trader, **James Magoffin**, who was married to Armijo's cousin. Kearny declared New Mexico a territory of the United States and installed Charles Bent as governor. (New Mexico Territory at that time included present-day Arizona.) The Mexican War ended in 1848 with the **Treaty of Guadalupe Hidalgo**. Mexico gave up all claims to Texas and ceded New Mexico and California to the United States in exchange for $15 million. The United States had gained some 529,000 square miles (1,370,100 square km) of new land and more than 20,000,000 new citizens.

In 1846, despite the ongoing war, more than a million dollars worth of goods were taken over the Santa Fe Trail, more than three times the value of the previous year. The American occupation of New Mexico opened the door even wider to trade. But it also aroused fears among New Mexicans that their lands might be seized. In January 1847, residents of Taos revolted, killing and scalping Governor Bent, who had moved to Taos. Twenty other Americans were also killed. The hostility spread to Plains tribes, who stepped up their attacks on caravans along the trail. More than 330 wagons were looted, 6,500 head of stock run off, and 47 members of trading parties killed. For the first time, Cheyenne and Arapaho groups attacked Bent's Fort.

SUSAN MAGOFFIN
One of the first European-American women to travel over the Santa Fe Trail was Susan Shelby Magoffin, who was 18 when she made the journey in 1846. Her diary, *Down the Santa Fe Trail and into Mexico*, tells the fascinating story of her 15-month trip. Susan was the sister-in-law of James Magoffin, who traveled to Santa Fe that year to negotiate the American takeover with General Armijo.

William Bent

BENT BURNS FORT

In August 1849, William Bent moved everything out of his fort and burned it down rather than sell it to the government for a price he considered too low. Today's Bent's Old Fort is a reconstruction, depicting life as it was in the mid-19th century on the American frontier. Bent moved his belongings 60 miles (97 km) to the east, where he built Bent's New Fort.

Re-enactment of soldiers firing a cannon at Fort Union, one of many military posts along the Santa Fe Trail

Between 1847 and 1865, the United States government spent more than $40 million to keep the Santa Fe Trail open. The United States cavalry helped defend the caravans from Indian attack, and new military posts appeared, especially along the Kansas-Oklahoma sections of the trail. After gold was discovered in California in 1848, settlers moving west used portions of the trail, and traffic continued to increase.

Gold miners headed for California are seen here loading a pack mule.

(Left) trader and writer Josiah Gregg

COMMERCE OF THE PRAIRIES

One trader, **Josiah Gregg**, traveled with many caravans, beginning in 1831. He wrote *Commerce of the Prairies*, published in 1844, which is still considered a classic book about the Santa Fe Trail. Gregg described the excitement of entering Santa Fe and documented his various journeys in detail.

Trading caravans continued on the Santa Fe Trail during the Civil War, from 1861 to 1865. Because of movements of soldiers along the trail, and an established mail service, traffic was heavy during those years. Between May 12 and July 12, 1865, the traffic count at one point included 2,692 people, 1,183 wagons, 736 horses, 2,904 mules, 15,855 oxen, and 56 carriages.

But by the end of 1866, use of the trail was declining. Two 19th century inventions–the steam engine and the railroad–were already turning prairie schooners into curiosities of the past.

THE CIVIL WAR

The Civil War (1861-1865) affected the Santa Fe Trail because Texas and Missouri were **Confederate** states while New Mexico, Kansas, and Colorado were **Union** states. Confederate and Union forces fought a six-hour battle at Glorieta Pass, west of Santa Fe, in 1862. The Union forces won and Confederates were forced to leave New Mexico. There were skirmishes on the Kansas-Missouri border but in general trade was not disturbed. In October 1864, Union troops defeated a Confederate force of about 15,000 soldiers in two battles near Kansas City, Missouri, one on the Big Blue River and the second at Westport. Those defeats ended the Confederate threat at the eastern end of the trail.

A Civil War soldier and his family

From 1863 to 1866, the first steel rails were built from Wyandotte, Kansas, on the Missouri River, to Junction City, Kansas, 100 miles (160 km) to the west. By 1872, the rails reached the point on the Arkansas River where Becknell had created the Cimarron Cutoff. In 1879, a tunnel was built to take passengers and freight over Raton Pass into New Mexico. And in February 1880, the first train rolled into Santa Fe. The Santa Fe newspaper, *The New Mexican*, ran a headline that read: "The Old Santa Fe Trail Passes Into Oblivion."

By 1890, much of the old trail was overgrown with grass and was largely forgotten. A few sections were still used for local traffic. But a book, *Stories of the Old Santa Fe Trail*, by a Kansas writer named **Henry Inman**, began to make readers curious. That book, published in 1881, and two later books he wrote created new interest in the trail's history and led to an effort to preserve its traces.

By the turn of the century the railroad had made use of the Santa Fe Trail almost unnecessary.

The Kansas State Historical Society and the Daughters of the American Revolution began a campaign to mark the Santa Fe Trail. A grant of $1,000 from the Kansas legislature in 1905 helped pay for 95 stone markers along the Kansas section. Most of these can still be seen today. Twenty-seven additional markers were placed along the mountain route and the Cimarron Cutoff, and one at the southeast corner of the central plaza in Santa Fe.

In 1987, Congress made the Santa Fe Trail a National Historic Trail. This act assures that its physical **remnants** and colorful history will be preserved for generations to come.

Marker from the central plaza in Santa Fe, marking the end of the trail

All that's left of some parts of the trail are signs placed along the way

FRANCIS AUBRY

Francis X. Aubry was the "fastest trader" on the Santa Fe Trail. In early 1848, he made the trip in only 8 days and 10 hours. Not content with that record, he bet $1,000 that he could top it. He left Santa Fe on September 12, 1848, racing between horses he had posted along the way, strapping himself to his horse to keep from falling off. His last horse dropped dead from exhaustion, so he hurried on foot to the Arkansas River, 20 miles (32 km) away. Borrowing a horse, he galloped off. When he staggered into the Merchants Hotel in Independence, he had made the ride in 5 days, 16 hours, and won his bet. Today, the trip takes about one and a half days by automobile.

Francis Aubry earned his nickname of "fastest trader."

KEY PEOPLE IN THE HISTORY OF *The Santa Fe Trail*

Armijo, Manuel - Mexican governor of New Mexico, who abandoned Santa Fe when U.S. troops entered in 1846.

Aubry, Francis X. (1824-1854) - Trader from Canada who made many trips over the Santa Fe Trail and broke speed records for covering the distance.

Baird, James - St. Louis blacksmith who, along with Samuel Chambers, dug "The Caches," to bury their goods for the winter on a trading mission in 1822.

Becknell, William (1796?-1865) - U.S. trader and explorer known as the "Father of the Santa Fe Trail."

Bent, Charles (1799-1847) - Trader born in West Virginia, who became the first U.S. governor of New Mexico.

Bent, William (1809-1869) - Brother of Charles Bent and founder of Bent's Fort in Colorado (1832).

Benton, Thomas Hart (1782-1858) - U.S. senator from Missouri.

Carson, Kit (1809-1868) - U.S. trapper, guide, and soldier.

Chambers, Samuel - U.S. trader who, along with James Baird, created the landmark known as "The Caches" in 1822 on the Arkansas River.

Chouteau, Auguste (1749-1829) - U.S. fur trader who founded the trading post that became St. Louis, Missouri.

Clark, William (1770-1838) - U.S. explorer who, along with Meriwether Lewis, led a famous exploration of the Louisiana Purchase (1804-1806).

Cooper, Stephen - U.S. trader who led many caravans to Santa Fe and brought back ancestors of the first "Missouri mules."

Gregg, Josiah (1806-1850) - Author of the two-volume *Commerce of the Prairies*.

Inman, Henry (1837-1899) - Kansas author of *Stories of the Old Santa Fe Trail*, 1881; *The Old Santa Fe Trail: The Story of a Great Highway*, 1897; and *Tales of the Trail: Short Stories of Western Life*, 1898.

Jackson, Andrew (1767-1845) - Seventh president of the U.S. (1829-1837).

Kearny, Stephen Watts (1774-1848) - U.S. general who took possession of New Mexico in 1846.

Lewis, Meriwether (1774-1809) - Secretary to President Jefferson and U.S. explorer who led, with William Clark, the first exploration of the Louisiana Purchase (1804-1806).

Magoffin, James (1799-1868) - Santa Fe trader who in 1846 convinced the New Mexican governor not to resist a U.S. takeover.

Magoffin, Susan Shelby (1828-1855) - Wife of Samuel Magoffin, who traveled with her husband on the Santa Fe Trail in 1846-1847. Her diary was later published as a book, *Down the Santa Fe Trail and into Mexico*.

Monroe, James (1758-1831) - Fifth president of the U.S. (1817-1825).

Pike, Zebulon (1779-1813) - U.S. explorer in the Louisiana Territory, Colorado, and New Mexico. Pikes Peak in Colorado was named after him.

Sibley, George (1782-1863) - Indian trader at Fort Osage, Missouri; one of three commissioners named in 1825 to survey the Santa Fe Trail.

Smith, Jedediah (1798-1831) - Mountain man and Indian fighter who guided caravans on the Santa Fe Trail.

St. Vrain, Ceran (1802-1870) - U.S. trader from Missouri who became Charles Bent's partner in a successful 19th century southwest trading company.

A Timeline of the History of
The Santa Fe Trail

1350   Taos Pueblo is built, and the Taos and other Pueblo peoples trade with nomadic Native tribes for several centuries, creating trails that become the eastern section of the Santa Fe Trail.

1610   Spain founds the capital city of Santa Fe in Nuevo Mexico.

1806   Zebulon Pike travels to New Mexico, is arrested and taken to Santa Fe and Chihuahua, and released.

1810   Pike publishes his report about the opportunities for trading in Santa Fe.

1812   Another trading party led by Robert McKnight travels to Santa Fe. The men are arrested and spend eight years in a Mexican prison.

1817   Chouteau party arrested in Taos. Furs are taken and they are jailed in Santa Fe, released a few months later.

1821   Becknell's caravan meets Mexican soldiers in New Mexico and is welcomed because Mexico has just won its independence from Spain.

1822   Baird/Chambers party has to bury their goods at the Arkansas River, creating a landmark on the Trail, "The Caches." Second Becknell caravan leaves the river at that point, pioneering the Cimarron Cutoff.

1825   President James Monroe orders a survey of the Santa Fe Trail.

1827-1831 Council Grove established as rendezvous point for caravans bound for Santa Fe.

1829 First caravan escorted by U.S. soldiers.

1834 William Bent builds Bent's Fort in southeastern Colorado.

1839 Governor Armijo of New Mexico increases taxes on caravans, forcing larger wagons and longer caravans.

1844 Publication of Josiah Gregg's *Commerce of the Prairies.*

1846-1848 The Mexican War, in which General Kearny captures Santa Fe.

1846-1847 Susan Magoffin is the first European-American woman on the Trail.

1848 Under the Treaty of Guadalupe Hidalgo, United States gains New Mexico, Arizona, and California. Francis Aubry sets speed record on the Trail.

1849 William Bent burns Bent's Old Fort and builds Bent's New Fort.

1861-1865 U.S. Civil War.

1863-1872 The first steel rails are built in Kansas and reach the Cimarron Cutoff.

1880 The first train rolls into Santa Fe.

1881 Publication of Henry Inman's *Stories of the Old Santa Fe Trail.*

1905 State of Kansas funds 95 stone markers along the Trail.

1987 U.S. Congress establishes the Santa Fe National Historic Trail.

GLOSSARY

adobe - A building material made of dried earth or clay and straw.

Apache - A number of Native American groups of the Southwest, originally from Canada, whose languages come from a language group called Athabascan.

artery - A vessel that carries blood from the heart; a major channel or route of transportation.

caravan - A company of travelers on a journey, especially in desert terrain.

Cheyenne - A number of Native American tribes of the U.S. western plains, whose language comes from the language group called Algonquian.

Comanche - A group of Native American nomadic people who ranged from Wyoming and Nebraska south into Texas and New Mexico, and who speak a Uto-Aztecan language.

company - Fellowship; a body of soldiers (several dozen individuals) usually consisting of a headquarters and two or three platoons.

Confederate - An alliance; denotes the southern states (the "South") that seceded from the U.S. in 1860 and 1861 and fought the Union Army (the "North") over the legality of slavery in the Civil War.

continental - Relating to a continent, especially the part of a country on a specific continent or land mass.

customs - The office of a country that imposes fees, or duties, on products entering or leaving the country.

division - One of the parts into which a whole is divided; a self-contained military unit capable of independent action such as conducting a battle.

empire - A major political unit with a large territory or a number of territories under a single power, especially if the leader is an emperor.

Kansas - The 34th state of the union; a Native American group that once lived in that area.

Kiowa - A Native American people from the present-day states of Colorado, Kansas, New Mexico, Oklahoma and Texas, who speak a common language called Kiowa.

lieutenant - An official who acts on behalf of a higher official; the leader of a subdivision of the overall group.

mountain man - An American frontiersman who usually began as a beaver trapper and often became an explorer, guide, trader, or settler.

offspring - A descendant, such as a child or young animal; a product or result of something else.

Osage - A Native American people originally from Missouri, who speak a Siouan language.

Pawnee - A Native American people originally from present-day Kansas or Nebraska.

Prairie schooner - Also called a "Santa Fe wagon." It had a bed that was 12 feet (3.66 m) long (15 feet [4.57 m] long on top) and 10 feet (3.05 m) high. With cotton sheets covering its "bows," it resembled a ship at sea.

Pueblo - "Village" or "people" in Spanish; a group of southwestern Native American peoples who traditionally farmed the Rio Grande Valley in New Mexico.

recession - A period of reduced economic activity.

remnants - Small parts or traces; a small surviving group.

rendezvous - From French, a place for assembling or meeting.

Sangre de Cristo Mountains - Southern Rocky Mountains in Colorado and New Mexico; Spanish for "blood of Christ."

skirmish - A minor fight in war or a minor dispute between opposing parties.

stockade - A line of strong posts or an enclosure, forming a defense.

Taos Pueblo - Northernmost of the Rio Grande Pueblos in north-central New Mexico, continuously inhabited for at least 700 years.

tariff - A duty or fee imposed by a government on imported or exported goods.

tax - A charge imposed by an authority on persons or property to raise money for public purposes.

territory - A geographical area; in the United States, an area under its control, with a separate legislature, but not yet a state.

The Caches - French for "hiding places"; the place where traders James Baird and William Chambers were forced to bury merchandise for the winter at the Arkansas River in 1822.

tongue - Referring to a wagon, the long, narrow piece, or pole, to which the draft animals are attached.

transcontinental - Extending across a continent, such as a railway.

Treaty of Guadalupe Hidalgo - The agreement that ended the Mexican War in 1848.

turret - Little tower at a corner or angle of a larger structure.

Union - The group of states that opposed slavery in the U.S. Civil War, while continuing to operate under the United States Constitution.

Ute - A Native American people originally inhabiting Utah, Colorado, Arizona, and New Mexico, speaking languages of the Uto-Aztecan language family.

watchtower - A tower for a lookout.

yoke - A wooden bar by which two draft animals are joined at the head for working together.

Books of Interest

Bacon, Melvin (Contributor). *Bent's Fort: Crossroad of Cultures on the Santa Fe Trail*, Millbrook Press, 1995

Bernstein, Vivian. *America's History: Land of Liberty/Book 2*, Steck-Vaughn Company, 1997.

Cantor, Carrie Nichols. *The Mexican War: How the United States Gained Its Western Lands*, Childs World, 2003.

Drumm, Stella., ed. *Down the Santa Fe Trail and into New Mexico: The Diary of Susan Shelby Magoffin*, University of Nebraska Press, 1982.

Gregg, Josiah. *Commerce of the Prairies*, University of Oklahoma Press, 1954.

Lavender, David Sievert. *The Santa Fe Trail*, Holiday House, 1995.

Russell, Marian. *Land of Enchantment, Memoirs along the Santa Fe Trail*, University of New Mexico Press, 1981.

Simmons, Marc. *Following the Santa Fe Trail: A Guide to the Modern Traveler*, Ancient City Press, 3rd edition, 2001.

Web Sites

http://www.ku.edu/heritage/research/sft/

http://www.nps.gov/safe/fnl-sft/broch/newbro.htm

http://www.santafelibrary.org/localhistory.html

For figuring today's equivalents of past prices: http://www.eh.net/hmit/compare/index.php

INDEX

Linda Thompson is a Montana native and a graduate of the University of Washington. She was a teacher, writer, and editor in the San Francisco Bay Area for 30 years and now lives in Taos, New Mexico. She can be contacted through her web site:

http://www.highmesaproductions.com